P9-DDW-090

A Question of Science

Why IS Ice slippery?

And other questions about MATERIALS

Anna Claybourne

CRABTREE PUBLISHING COMPANY
WWW.CRABTREEBOOKS.COM

CRABTREE
PUBLISHING COMPANY
WWW.CRABTREEBOOKS.COM

Published in Canada
Crabtree Publishing
616 Welland Ave.
St. Catharines, Ontario
L2M 5V6

Published in the United States
Crabtree Publishing
347 Fifth Avenue
Suite 1402–145
New York, NY 10016

Published in 2021 by Crabtree Publishing Company

First published in 2020 by Wayland
© Hodder and Stoughton 2020

Author: Anna Claybourne

Editorial Director: Kathy Middleton

Editor: Julia Bird

Proofreader: Petrice Custance

Design and illustration: Matt Lilly

Cover design: Matt Lilly

Production coordinator and
  Prepress technician: Tammy McGarr

Print coordinator: Katherine Berti

Printed in the U.S.A./082020/CG20200601

Picture credits
Dreamstime: Eknarin Maphichai 17tl; Felix Pergande 25c.
Science Photo Library: Natural History Museum London 19b; Javier Trueba/MSF 19c.
Shutterstock: Africa Studio 17tr, 20tl, 22clr, 22cr; Waqar Ahmed 86 18t; Tommy Alven 21t; Willyam Bradberry 26t; Captureandcompose 4bl; Chones 21t 26-27; Marcel Clemens 12br; CWIS 15t; Demidoff 27c; Djgis 26c; Dimmber 6cl; George Dolgikh 12cr; Domnitsky 4c; Dreamsquare 22br; Angela Dukich 25t; Engraving Factory 4bc; Fotokostic 20cl; Hekla 28t; Anton Herrington 23b; Hidesy 8c; Hortimages 10b; Palmer Kane LLC 16cl; Kertu 28b; Chris Kolaczan 19t; Peter Kotoff 29t; Olha Kozachenko 17b; Gita Kulinitch Studio 4bcr; Andrey_Kuzmin 4cl, 8t, 10t, 22cl; Macrowildlife 4cr; Alexander Mak 27l; mamma_mia 20cr; MIA Studio 16cr; Militarist 5tr; Nattika 21cr; Nyura 18c; Mike_O 22clc; Hoha-OLD 6t; Patpitchaya 29c; Picador Pictures 17cr; Kittiphong Phongaen 4br; Photka 4clc; Photographicss 4bcl; rCarner 8b; Will Rodrigues 9t; Sashkin 22bc; Sebastian Studio 18b; Snehit Photo 5l; Sportpoint 6cr; Bernhard Staehli 25b; Sunny Forest 12bl; Angelus_Svetlana 27r; TaraPatta 21cl; Igor Tarasyuk 12c; TravnikovStudio 4t; Vector Pattern 17c; WDG Photo 24; Xpixel 17cl, 21b, 26b; Vasilyev: 19t; Yeti studio 1,12cl.

Library and Achives Canada Cataloguing in Publication

Title: Why is ice slippery? : and other questions about materials / Anna Claybourne.
Names: Claybourne, Anna, author.
Description: Series statement: A question of science | Includes index.
Identifiers: Canadiana (print) 20200255851 | Canadiana (ebook) 20200255878 | ISBN 9780778779407 (softcover) | ISBN 9780778777489 (hardcover) | ISBN 9781427125446 (PDF)
Subjects: LCSH: Matter—Juvenile literature. | LCSH: Matter—Miscellanea—Juvenile literature. | LCGFT: Trivia and miscellanea.
Classification: LCC QC173.16 .C53 2020 | DDC j530.4—dc23

Library of Congress Cataloging-in-Publication Data

Names: Claybourne, Anna, author.
Title: Why is ice slippery? : and other questions about materials / Anna Claybourne.
Description: New York, NY : Crabtree Publishing Company, 2021. | Series: A question of science | First published in 2020 by Wayland.
Identifiers: LCCN 2020023606 (print) | LCCN 2020023607 (ebook) | ISBN 9780778777489 (hardcover) | ISBN 9780778779407 (paperback) | ISBN 9781427125446 (ebook)
Subjects: LCSH: Materials--Juvenile literature.
Classification: LCC TA403.2 .C535 2021 (print) | LCC TA403.2 (ebook) | DDC 670--dc23
LC record available at https://lccn.loc.gov/2020023606
LC ebook record available at https://lccn.loc.gov/2020023607

Contents

What are materials?

Reach out and feel whatever's around you. Is it a book, your clothes, a chair or sofa, a snack? Or maybe you're on a beach, surrounded by rocks and sand. Well, wherever you are, you wouldn't be there if it weren't for materials.

Rock

Water

Sand

Cotton

Without materials, you'd have nothing to sit on, wear, or touch. You wouldn't have this book. But that wouldn't matter much because you wouldn't exist either!

Materials = STUFF

Materials are, quite simply, the STUFF that everything is made from. There are millions of different types of materials.

Here are just some of them...

Materials in nature

Water

Rock

Soil

Gold

Living materials that grow

Bone

Eggshell

Wood

Cotton

Wool

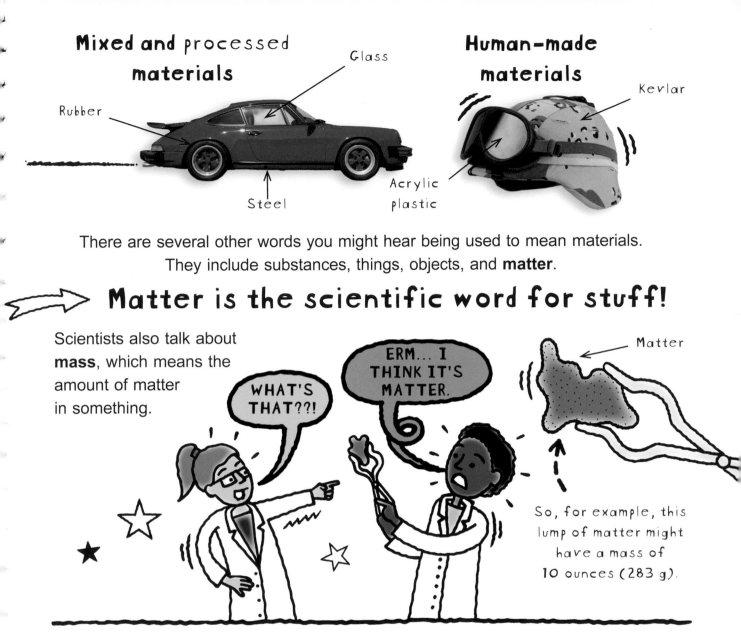

Mixed and processed materials

Glass

Rubber

Steel

Human-made materials

Kevlar

Acrylic plastic

There are several other words you might hear being used to mean materials. They include substances, things, objects, and **matter**.

⟹ **Matter is the scientific word for stuff!**

Scientists also talk about **mass**, which means the amount of matter in something.

WHAT'S THAT??!

ERM... I THINK IT'S MATTER.

Matter

So, for example, this lump of matter might have a mass of 10 ounces (283 g).

Material world

Materials make up everything around us: our planet, our homes, our food, even ourselves. So we need to understand how different materials work, change, and behave, and what they are useful for in order to survive.

Since humans first existed, we've been exploring and experimenting with materials to see what they can do and how we can use them. We are constantly asking questions about them.

This book will try to answer some of them!

5

What is everything made of?

That's a good question!
(And it's something that you would expect scientists to have discovered by now.)
But it's actually quite hard to answer.

AHEM! WE'RE NOT QUITE SURE.

We DO know this much...

Materials are made of tiny units called **atoms**.

Atoms that are tightly packed together and do not move make a thing SOLID.

In a liquid, atoms can move and flow.

In a gas, atoms are more spread out.

Building blocks

There are different types of atoms, and each type forms an element, or a pure material. Elements are the building blocks of matter. The element gold is made of gold atoms.

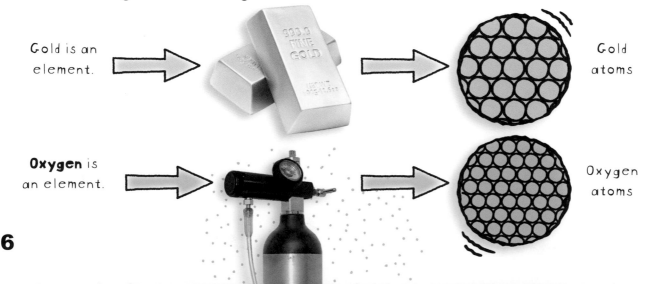

Gold is an element.

Gold atoms

Oxygen is an element.

Oxygen atoms

Compounds

Different atoms can also combine to make **molecules**, which make up other materials. Materials made from molecules are called **compounds**.

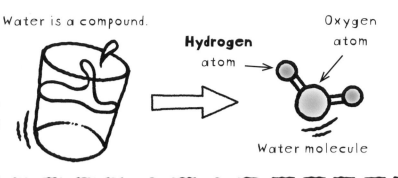

Water is a compound.

Hydrogen atom → Oxygen atom

Water molecule

Mixture

And elements and compounds can also mix together to make even more materials. A material made of other, mixed materials is called... a mixture!

mud

Mud is a mixture.

Mud is made of water mixed with **particles** of rock.

Smaller and smaller...

Atoms are made of even tinier particles, called protons, neutrons, and electrons. And they are made of EVEN tinier ones, such as quarks and leptons.

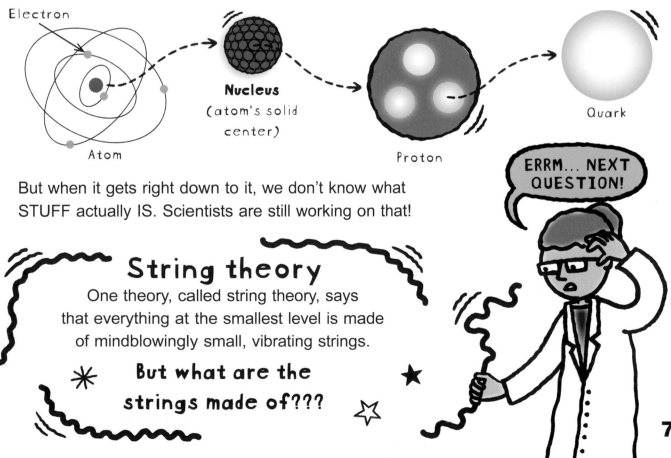

Electron

Atom

Nucleus
(atom's solid center)

Proton

Quark

But when it gets right down to it, we don't know what STUFF actually IS. Scientists are still working on that!

String theory

One theory, called string theory, says that everything at the smallest level is made of mindblowingly small, vibrating strings.

But what are the strings made of???

ERRM... NEXT QUESTION!

7

How big are atoms and molecules?

However closely you look at something, you can't see the individual atoms it's made of. That's because they are so INCREDIBLY tiny.

One single atom

Too small to see!

A typical atom is roughly 0.0000001 mm across. That's one 10-millionth of a millimeter.

A page in a book is about a million atoms thick.

You could fit about 2,500 million atoms on your little fingernail…

… and a glass of water contains about 24 **SEPTILLION** atoms.

A septillion is a million million million million.

So that's 24,000,000,000,000,000,000,000,000 atoms in a glass of water. That's more than the number of glasses of water in the sea.

Empty space

An atom isn't a solid ball. It has a solid center, called the nucleus, with tiny parts called electrons zooming around it.

Electron   Nucleus

In diagrams such as this, the nucleus looks quite big, so that you can see it. But it's actually tiny. If the whole atom was the size of a football stadium…

… the nucleus would be the size of a pea!

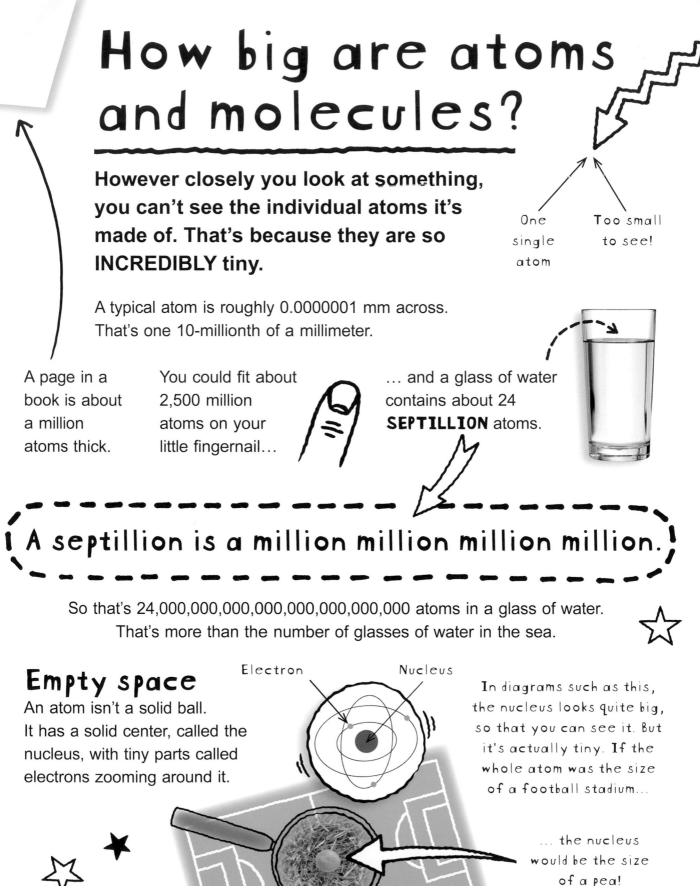

You're mostly nothing!

This means that most of an atom is actually not made of matter. It is a space that's filled only by a cloud of tiny, high-energy electrons.

If you could squash all the matter in your body down so that there was no empty space in the atoms, you'd be smaller than a grain of salt.

Helium

Gold

Carbon

Big and small

Different kinds of atoms contain different numbers of particles. That makes some heavier and bigger than others.

Making molecules

Molecules are made up of atoms joined together. Some are small, such as a water molecule, which has three atoms: two hydrogen atoms and one oxygen atom.

Some are bigger, such as this molecule of fructose, a type of sugar found in fruit.

This is what makes a strawberry taste sweet!

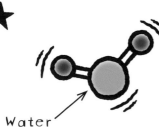

Water molecule

Fructose molecule

What are those sticks for?

Diagrams and models of molecules often show the atoms joined together with sticks so you can see each part clearly.

In fact, a molecule is more like this, with the atoms squished together.

Water molecule

Why is ice slippery?

Materials exist in three main **states**:
SOLID, **LIQUID**, and GAS.
The solid state of water is ice.
We all know ice can be very slippery.
But why is that?

DON'T FALL OVER!

Ice mystery

We're used to ice being slippery, but finding out what makes it slippery hasn't been easy. In fact, for a long time, scientists have got it wrong. Here are the WRONG answers!

① Standing on ice makes it melt.

WRONG!

It is true that **pressure** can lower the freezing temperature of ice and make it start to melt. So scientists thought that standing on ice melted the surface into a layer of water, making you slide and slip along. However, it actually takes a LOT of pressure to do this—much more than a human's weight. So that's not the answer.

② Friction heats the ice and makes it melt.

WRONG!

Friction happens when surfaces rub together, and it creates heat.
(For example, when you rub your hands together to warm them up.)
So another idea was the friction created by skating or sliding around on ice made it melt. This can happen when ice skaters are moving fast. But ice is slippery even when you're standing still. So it's not that either!

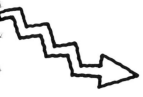

And if you think about it, why should ice melting into water make it so slippery? A wet floor or wet rocks can be a bit slippery but nowhere near as slippery as ice.

So what IS the answer?

Rolling around

The latest theory is that on the surface, some of the molecules that make up the ice break free.

In ice, water molecules are joined together in a fixed grid or **lattice**.

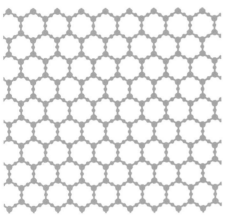

But at the surface, some molecules can break off

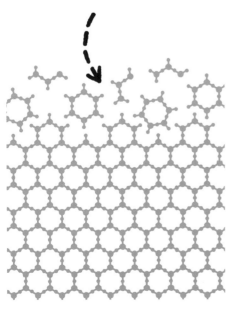

The loose molecules roll and skid around on the surface, like ball bearings on a smooth floor...

WHOOPS!

... making the ice very hard to grip!

And did you know?

When ice is really cold, below about -40°F (-40°C), it's not slippery!

11

Why is air invisible?

Air is all around us. It's made up of gases.
Gases are materials. So why can't we see air?

What is a gas?

Gas is one of the three states of matter. The state a material is in depends on its temperature.

Solid

Molecules are fixed together but jiggle around.

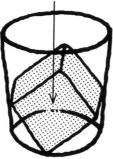

Solids keep their shape.

Liquid

Molecules have more energy and move faster.

Liquids can flow and change shape.

Gas

The molecules move so fast, they zoom around at high speeds.

They ping away from each other and spread out.

As a solid gets warmer, it melts into a liquid.

As a liquid gets warmer, it **evaporates** into a gas.

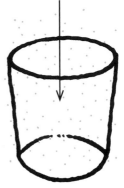

How hot?

You probably know that water freezes into solid ice at 32°F (0°C), and boils into steam (a gas) at 212°F (100°C). But other materials change states at other temperatures.

Chocolate melts at about 90°F (32°C).

The metal mercury is liquid at room temperature, but freezes solid at about -38°F (-39°C).

Gases in the air

Air is mostly made of the elements oxygen and **nitrogen**. At the temperatures we have on Earth, they are normally gases.

Tiny amounts of other gases, such as: argon, **carbon dioxide**, and water vapor

Because they are gases, the tiny molecules zoom around at high speeds, with big spaces in between. Each molecule is too small to see on its own, so the gas is invisible.

Nitrogen

COMING THROUGH!

Water vapor

Oxygen

Carbon dioxide

WATCH OUT!

Ingredients of air

Oxygen gas: about 21%

Nitrogen gas: about 78%

Solid air

Air can be liquid and even solid. Liquid air looks like water.

It becomes liquid at a mindbogglingly cold -328°F (-200°C)

... and freezes solid at an even chillier -364°F (-220°C)!

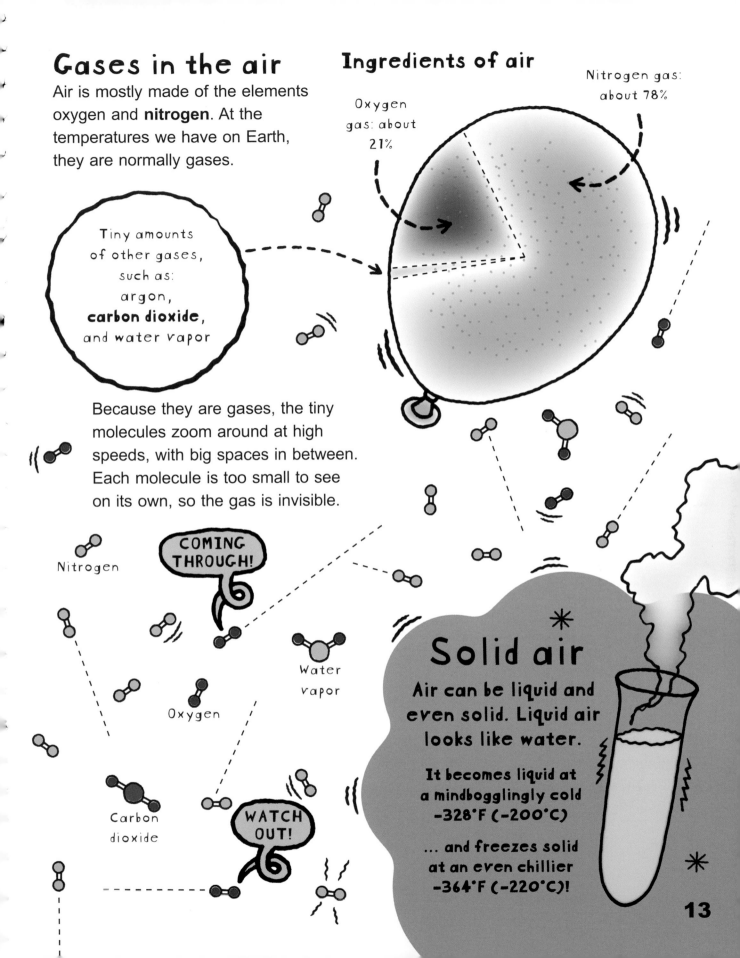

13

Is human hair really as strong as steel?

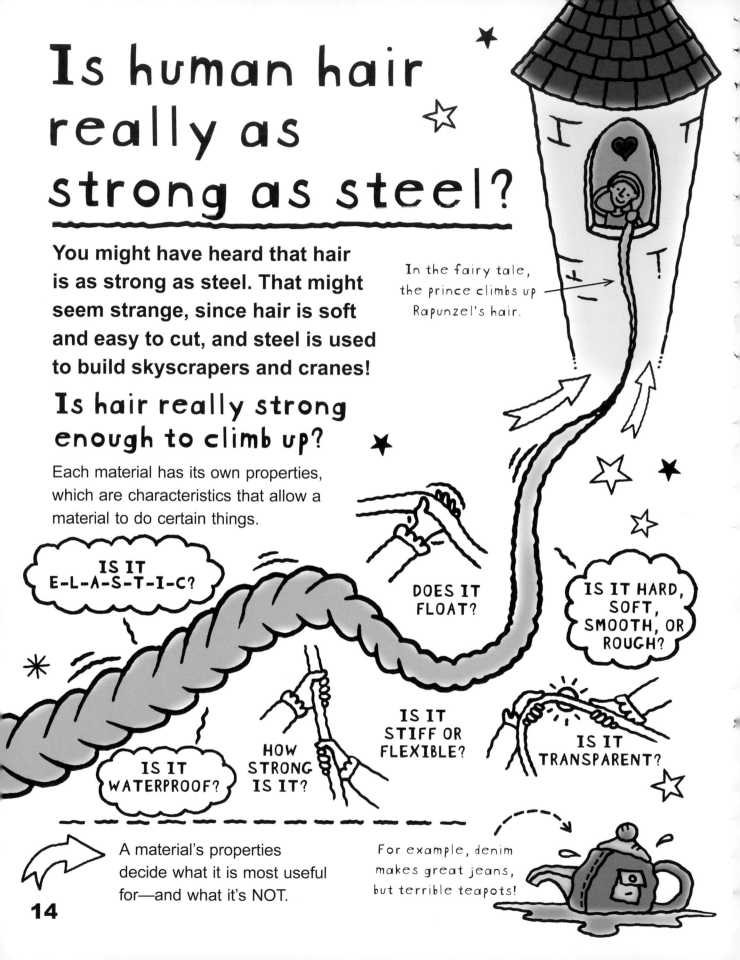

You might have heard that hair is as strong as steel. That might seem strange, since hair is soft and easy to cut, and steel is used to build skyscrapers and cranes!

In the fairy tale, the prince climbs up Rapunzel's hair.

Is hair really strong enough to climb up?

Each material has its own properties, which are characteristics that allow a material to do certain things.

IS IT E-L-A-S-T-I-C?

DOES IT FLOAT?

IS IT HARD, SOFT, SMOOTH, OR ROUGH?

IS IT WATERPROOF?

HOW STRONG IS IT?

IS IT STIFF OR FLEXIBLE?

IS IT TRANSPARENT?

A material's properties decide what it is most useful for—and what it's NOT.

For example, denim makes great jeans, but terrible teapots!

14

Hair strength test

Strength is an important property, because all kinds of things need to be strong, from buildings and bridges to pots and sewing thread.

This strength test measures how much weight a strand of material can hold before it breaks. Scientists who deal with materials often do strength tests.

Weights are suspended from the strands to see how much they can hold.

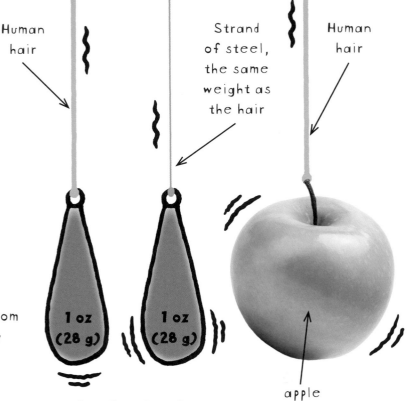

Human hair

Strand of steel, the same weight as the hair

Human hair

1 oz (28 g)

1 oz (28 g)

apple 3.5 oz (100 g)

Which wins?

In this test, the hair would do pretty well. An average human hair can hold about 3.5 oz (100 g)—the weight of a large apple. It's not quite as strong as steel, but it IS as strong as some other metals, such as aluminum.

On average, people have about 100,000 hairs on their heads. If one hair can hold an apple, a whole head of hair could support the weight of two elephants!

(Hair roots are NOT that strong though, so don't try dangling elephants off your hair at home.)

Stretch, don't squish

This pulling strength is called tensile strength. However, this is only one type of strength. Scientists also test compressive strength, which means how strong something is when it's squashed.

On that test, steel is much stronger than human hair.

Why does salt disappear in water?

Put a spoonful of salt into a glass of water, stir it, and –

Ta-daaaa!

It vanishes!

The water looks just like normal water. Try it with a spoonful of sugar, too, and the same thing will happen.

Taste test

You can prove the sugar and salt are still there by tasting them. Don't drink the whole glass, though. Just dip your finger in and dab a bit on your tongue.

BLAH–SALTY!

MMM–SWEET!

Salt, sugar, and many other materials **dissolve** in water. The water breaks them down into tiny molecules, or sometimes even atoms.

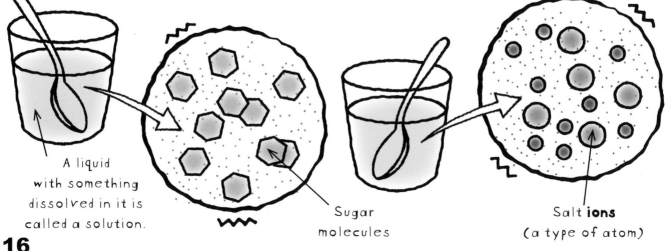

A liquid with something dissolved in it is called a solution.

Sugar molecules

Salt **ions** (a type of atom)

Does everything dissolve in water?
NO. A lot of materials do dissolve in water, but some don't.

Sugar and salt do.

Some types of rock do, such as limestone and chalk.

Limestone caves are hollowed out by water dissolving the rock.

Things that don't dissolve in water include candle wax, gold, and rubber.

Other solvents

Some things, such as nail polish, don't dissolve in water, but will dissolve in another liquid!

Nail polish will not dissolve in water, so it doesn't come off in the shower or swimming pool.

You can only remove it with nail polish remover. Remover contains a different **solvent**, such as ethyl acetate, which dissolves the nail polish.

Get it back!

If you've dissolved salt or sugar in water, you can get it out again.

Pour some of the solution onto a plate or saucer.

Leave it somewhere warm, such as a sunny windowsill.

The water will evaporate, leaving the salt or sugar behind.

17

Where do crystals come from?

Crystals include rare and valuable materials, such as diamonds, as well as some of the most common materials, such as salt, sugar, water, and ice.

Crystal shapes

In a crystal, the molecules fit together in a pattern that repeats all the way through. This gives the crystal a particular shape based on the shape of the molecules.

Here's an example: table salt.

Salt molecules are made up of two types of atoms:

Sodium   Chlorine

They fit together in a cube-shaped molecule...

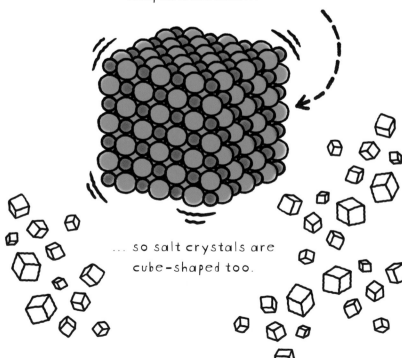

... so salt crystals are cube-shaped too.

Diamonds

Jadeite

Sugar crystals

How can crystals grow?

Crystals aren't alive, but they do grow. This happens when more and more atoms or molecules join onto the crystal in the same pattern.

Crystals can form when rock is melted, then cools again. For example, diamonds grow in magma, or melted rock, deep underground.

Magma

Diamond crystals

Carbon atoms join together in a crystal pattern.

Grow your own!

Crystals can also grow when a material is dissolved in water. You can grow a salt crystal like this:

Stir salt into a jar of hot water until it's finished dissolving. Tie a paperclip to a piece of string and tie the other end around a pencil. Lower the paper clip end into the water and balance the pencil across the top of the jar.

Leave it for a few days, and crystals should grow.

Cool crystals

In 2000, miners discovered a cave deep underground, filled with giant selenite crystals up to 39 feet (12 m) long and 3 feet (1 m) wide. That's huge!

Snowflakes are crystals. They have six points because they grow from six-sided molecules of ice.

When you look through a clear Iceland spar crystal, everything looks double!

19

Why do eggs go solid when you cook them? ☆

As you know, materials can melt into liquid as they heat up and freeze solid as they get colder. You can see this happening with things such as water, butter, and chocolate.

But some materials seem to break these rules.

Heat up a runny, liquid egg in a pan...

... and it turns hard and solid!

And what about toast? When you stick bread in a toaster, it doesn't melt.

It just gets darker and crispier.

What's going on?

Materials such as bread and eggs (and many other foods) contain **complicated** mixtures of **chemicals**. When they are heated, they **react** and change.

Eggs contain coiled-up strings of chemicals called proteins.

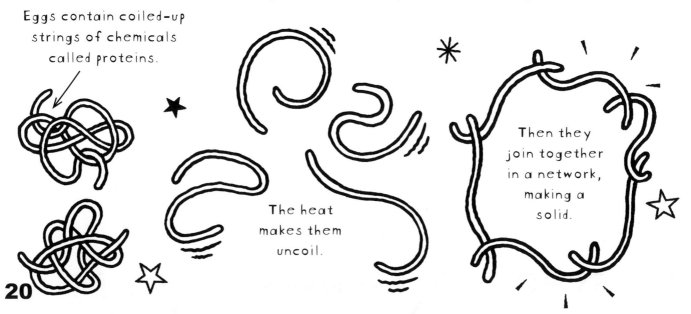

The heat makes them uncoil.

Then they join together in a network, making a solid.

Bread contains **carbohydrate** chemicals.

When they get heated, they start to burn, releasing carbon.

The carbon looks black, so the toast gets darker.

If you kept heating it, it would catch fire!

OUCH!

No going back!

On top of that, you can't undo these changes. You can't un-fry an egg or un-toast a slice of bread, because the chemicals have changed permanently. In science, these are called irreversible changes.

Freezing water is a reversible change, because you can undo it.

When you take a popsicle out of the freezer, the water in it will melt.

But cooking an egg is an irreversible change.

This egg is cooked forever!

The materials in eggs and bread could change states and melt, or turn into gas, if they got hot enough. But they never reach those states because we don't like to eat burned toast.

Also, if all food did melt or become gas, cooking would be very different. Everything would just melt into soup…

IT'S EVERYTHING SOUP AGAIN!

Thankfully, some things can burn for long periods without changing state. That's why we can make fires, light candles, and make engines work by burning fuel.

Why does metal feel cold?

Take a metal spoon out of a kitchen drawer, hold it against your arm, and it feels cold. But a wool sock feels warm—even if the sock and spoon are exactly the same temperature.

Chilly

Cozy!

FEELS COLD!

Putting your hand in a glass of water

Holding a smooth pebble

Jelly

FEELS WARM!

Wooden spoon

Fluffy cushion

Styrofoam packaging

But WHY?

When you touch a material, you're not actually feeling its temperature. You're sensing whether your skin is losing or gaining heat from touching it.

Here's how it works

① The spoon is at room temperature —about 68°F (20°C). Your skin is warmer, since body temperature is about 98.6°F (37°C).

② Metal is a very good **conductor** of heat. When it touches you, heat quickly spreads from your hand into the metal.

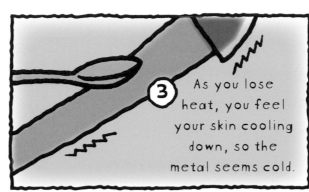

③ As you lose heat, you feel your skin cooling down, so the metal seems cold.

④

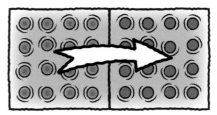

A wool sock is not good at conducting heat. Instead of carrying heat away, it stops your body heat from escaping, so your skin warms up.

Passing on heat

In hotter materials, the molecules have more energy and move around more.

When a warm material touches a cooler one, its faster molecules hit the slower molecules and make them speed up. That's how heat spreads from one object into another.

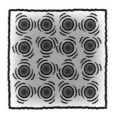

Warm object

Cooler object

Heat spreading

Materials that are good heat conductors quickly "suck" heat away from your skin, so they make you feel cold.

Good and bad

Metals are very good heat conductors. Water, glass, and stone are good conductors, too. So is anything wet, such as jelly.

Air is a poor conductor. Materials that feel warm and cozy usually contain trapped air, such as a sweater or Styrofoam.

To keep warm, we make duvets out of soft fabric and fluffy stuffing, not jelly!

SNUGGLY!

What makes the Eiffel Tower grow taller?

Living things, such as a sunflower or a kitten, grow. You grow. Even clouds and crystals can grow (see pages 18–19), although they're not alive.

But how can metal grow?

The Eiffel Tower is a famous iron tower in Paris, France. It's 1,063 feet (324 m) tall in the winter. But in the summer, especially on a hot day, it can be up to 6.7 inches (17 cm) taller.

6.7 inches (17 cm)

What's going on!?

This happens because most materials, especially metals, get bigger as they get warmer. It's called heat expansion.

A small piece of iron would only get slightly longer, not enough for you to notice. But a 1,063-foot (324-m) tall iron tower expands enough to make a difference you can measure easily.

Inside an iron bar, the molecules jiggle around.

As the molecules get hotter, they jiggle more and push against each other. This makes the piece of iron expand, or grow bigger.

Space to grow

It's not so bad for the Eiffel Tower, as it can just grow into the air. But what if a bridge gets longer in the heat?

Expansion joint

Good!

Not good!

That's why bridges and other big structures have gaps built into them, called expansion joints, to let each section grow in the heat.

Liquids and gases

Heat expansion happens in liquids and gases, too. In fact, they grow even more than solids. That's how a thermometer works!

A thermometer has liquid inside. As the temperature rises and falls, the liquid expands and shrinks.

Balloon trick

Growing oceans

Global warming is the gradual heating up of Earth. It has caused glaciers to melt faster. This extra water is making sea levels rise. But another reason they are rising is because water expands as it gets warmer and takes up more space.

See air expanding for yourself! Stretch a balloon over the neck of an empty plastic bottle. Then hold the bottle in a bowl of hot tap water.

The air inside expands and fills the balloon.

25

Do plastic bags last forever?

As you probably know, plastic bags are a BIG problem. Many end up as litter on the land and in the sea where they stay for a long, long time.

How long do they last?

It's hard to be sure, because plastic was only invented about 150 years ago. It's incredibly long-lasting, and doesn't break down like natural materials do. So we're not sure how long plastic bags might last. It could be thousands of years!

Sea creatures can die when they swallow plastic bags, mistaking them for food such as jellyfish.

A lot of rot

When things biodegrade, or rot, they are actually being eaten and digested by **bacteria**, which turn them into natural chemicals.

An apple rots after a few days.

Wood eventually decays.

Plastic bags don't!

Why doesn't it rot?

Although it's made from natural materials, such as oil from under the ground, plastic is a synthetic material. That means it is made by humans.

Oil is a fossil fuel made from the bodies of tiny ancient animals.

To make plastic, we take chemicals out of the oil and heat them up so that their molecules change.

Oil

Small molecules called **monomers**...

... join together to make very strong, long, molecule chains called **polymers**.

The GOOD NEWS is...

As a material, plastic has amazingly useful properties.

Flexible

Cheap

Waterproof

Strong

Long-lasting

Light

That's why we use it so much!

The BAD NEWS is...

The polymer molecules in plastic are too big and strong for bacteria to digest. That's why it doesn't break down and rot away. It can break up into smaller pieces, but they're still plastic and can harm animals and the environment.

What can we do?

HELP!

Invent alternative plastics that do rot away.

Find ways to collect and clean up waste plastic.

Breed **bacteria** that can digest plastic.

Meanwhile, it's a good idea to avoid using plastic if you can, especially plastic bags!

Quick-fire questions

Where does water go when it dries?

The water in a puddle in the sunshine, or in wet clothes hung up to dry, gradually disappears until it's all gone. Water turns into a gas when it boils. Even when it's not boiling, water molecules gradually break free into the air and become water vapor (water in the form of gas). The warmer it is, the faster the water molecules move and the more easily they break away, so things dry faster.

Why does ice float?

Most materials expand or grow as they get warmer, and shrink as they get colder. However, water is different. Below 39.2°F (4°C), water stops shrinking as it cools, and starts to grow again. Its molecules move away from each other slightly to form ice crystals. This means ice is less **dense** (lighter for its size) than liquid water, so it floats.

If lead is poisonous, why is it used in pencils?

Lead is a poisonous metal that can be very dangerous if you swallow it or breathe it into your lungs. However, the "lead" in pencils is not made of lead. It is made of graphite, a type of carbon (like the black stuff on burned toast). It's called lead because it looks similar, and when it was first discovered, people thought graphite was a type of lead.

How can pants be made of wood?

The fabrics we use to make clothes come from many different sources. Cotton and linen plants and animal wool have fibers that can be woven into cloth. We can also make cloth fibers from plastic. And some are made by processing wood or bamboo, which results in fabrics such as rayon and viscose.

How do clouds stay up?

Clouds are made of water, which is denser than air and doesn't float. But when water is in a gas form, as it is in clouds, its molecules are separate and zoom around very fast, just like all the other gases in the air. As the air cools, the water molecules start to stick together to make larger droplets, but they are still light enough to stay in the air.

Glossary

atoms Tiny units that matter is made up of

bacteria Tiny living things that feed on some types of matter

breed To mate certain animals in order to produce specific characteristics in the offspring

carbohydrate A food group that contains sugars and starches

carbon An important element found in living things

carbon dioxide A gas found in the air

chemical A substance that cannot be broken down into different parts

complicated Not easy to learn or understand

compounds Materials made from atoms of different elements joined together to form molecules

conductor A material that carries heat easily

crystals Materials with their atoms or molecules arranged in a regular repeating grid or lattice

dense How heavy something is for its size

dissolve To break up and disappear into a liquid

evaporates Changes from a liquid into a gas

friction A force that slows down or stops objects as they scrape or rub together

helium A type of gas that does not burn

hydrogen A common element, and one of the two ingredients of water

ions Atoms or molecules with an electric charge

lattice A regular pattern or grid of molecules found in some materials

mass The amount of matter that an object contains

matter The stuff that everything is made up of

molecules Units of matter made from atoms joined together

monomers Small single molecules that can join together to make larger molecules

nitrogen An element usually found as a gas, that makes up most of the air

nucleus The solid central part of an atom

oxygen A gas found in the air, and one of the two ingredients of water

particles Units that make up atoms

polymers Types of molecules made of a chain of monomers, and found in plastics

pressure The force of one thing pressing on another

processed Changed a material to achieve a particular result

react A chemical change that happens when elements combine

solvent A substance that dissolves another

states The forms in which materials can exist: solid, liquid, and gas

water vapor Water in the form of a gas

Learning More

Books

Biskup, Agnieszka. *The Solid Truth about States of Matter with Max Axiom, Super Scientist*. Capstone Press, 2019.

Claybourne, Anna. *Recreate Discoveries About States of Matter.* Crabtree Publishing, 2019.

Maurer, Tracy. *Atoms and Molecules.* Rourke Educational Media, 2012.

Sjonger, Rebecca. *Testing Materials in My Makerspace.* Crabtree Publishing, 2018.

Websites

www.exploratorium.edu/snacks/ subject/materials-and-matter
Matter and materials experiments from the Exploratorium.

www.dkfindout.com/us/science/ materials/
Matter and materials facts, pictures, and quizzes.

http://phet.colorado.edu/sims/html/ states-of-matter/latest/states-of-matter_ en.html
Interactive animation that lets you heat and cool materials to see what happens.

www.stevespanglerscience.com/lab/ categories/experiments states-of-matter/
States of matter experiments from Steve Spangler Science.

https://pt.kle.cz/en_US/index.html
The periodic table, a table showing all the elements.

Index